W9-BXE-800

First Facts®

First Cookbooks

A Pirate COOKBOOK

Simple Recipes for Kids

by Sarah L. Schuette

CAPSTONE PRESS
a capstone imprint

First Facts is published by Capstone Press,
151 Good Counsel Drive, P.O. Box 669, Mankato, Minnesota 56002.
www.capstonepub.com

 Books published by Capstone Press are manufactured with paper
containing at least 10 percent post-consumer waste.

Library of Congress Cataloging-in-Publication Data
Schuette, Sarah L., 1976-
  A pirate cookbook : simple recipes for kids / by Sarah L. Schuette.
    p. cm.—(First facts. First cookbooks)
  Summary: "Provides instructions and close-up step photos for making a variety of simple snacks and
drinks with a pirate theme"—Provided by publisher.
  Includes bibliographical references and index.
  ISBN 978-1-4296-5375-6 (library binding)
1. Cooking—Juvenile literature. I. Title. II. Series.

  TX652.5.S3437 2011
  641.5'123—dc22

                            2010028139

Editorial Credits
Lori Shores, editor; Juliette Peters, designer; Sarah Schuette, photo stylist; Marcy Morin, studio scheduler;
    Laura Manthe, production specialist

Photo Credits
All photos by Capstone Studio/Karon Dubke

The author dedicates this book in memory of her father, Willmar "Butch" Schuette.

Printed in the United States of America in North Mankato, Minnesota.
022011
006078R

Table of Contents

Pirate Pleasers

Hunting for treasure made pirates mighty hungry. Imagine your kitchen as a ship's **galley**, and make some pirate treats. These snacks are as good as gold when you make them yourself.

First take off your eye patch and read over each recipe. Then look in your cupboards for the tools and **ingredients** you'll need. If you have questions, just ask an adult.

Pirates were dirty, but you know better! Wash your hands before you start and put on an apron. And don't forget to clean up after yourself. Even pirates had to **swab** the deck!

Metric Conversion Chart	
United States	**Metric**
¼ teaspoon	1.2 mL
½ teaspoon	2.5 mL
1 teaspoon	5 mL
1 tablespoon	15 mL
¼ cup	60 mL
⅓ cup	80 mL
½ cup	120 mL
⅔ cup	160 mL
¾ cup	175 mL
1 cup	240 mL
1 ounce	30 gms

5

Tools

Pirates used tools like maps and **spyglasses** to find treasure. Use this handy guide to track down the tools you'll need.

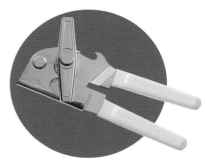

can opener—a tool used to open metal cans

cutting board—a wooden or plastic board used when slicing or chopping foods

ladle—a large deep spoon with a long handle used for serving soup

liquid measuring cup—a glass or plastic measuring cup with a spout for pouring

measuring cups—round, flat cups with handles used for measuring dry ingredients

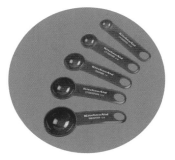

measuring spoons—spoons with small deep scoops used to measure both wet and dry ingredients

microwave-safe bowl—a non-metal bowl used to heat ingredients in a microwave oven

mixing bowl—a sturdy bowl used for mixing ingredients

pot holder—a thick, heavy fabric cut into a square or circle that is used to handle hot items

Techniques

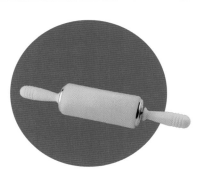

rolling pin—a tool used to flatten dough or to crush ingredients

strainer—a bowl-shaped tool with holes in the sides and bottom

whisk—a metal tool used for beating or stirring ingredients

crush—to squash something under a heavy weight

drain—to remove the liquid from something

mash—to crush food into a soft mixture

measure—to take a specific amount of something

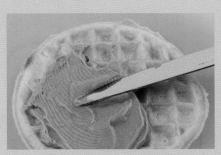

spread—to cover a surface with something

sprinkle—to scatter something in small drops or bits

stir—to mix something by moving a spoon around in it

whisk—to quickly stir one ingredient into another with a whisk

Gangplank Dippers

Pirates took a big dip in the ocean if they fell off the **gangplank**. Your dippers will taste much better than a mouthful of salt water.

Makes 12 dippers

Ingredients:
- 1 jar pizza sauce, 14 ounces
- ½ cup shredded mozzarella cheese
- 12 breadsticks

Tools:
- microwave-safe bowl
- plastic wrap
- microwave oven
- pot holders
- spoon
- measuring cups

1 Pour sauce into a microwave-safe bowl. Cover the bowl with plastic wrap.

2 Have an adult help you heat the sauce in microwave oven for 45 seconds.

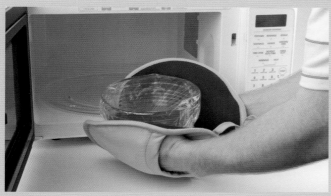

3 Ask an adult to help you take the bowl out of the microwave. Use pot holders to handle the hot bowl.

4 Remove plastic wrap. Stir the sauce with a spoon.

5 Measure cheese. Sprinkle it over the sauce.

6 Dip breadsticks into the sauce and cheese.

Chocolate Gunpowder

Gunpowder was like gold to pirates. The more they had, the more they could fire their **cannons**. This dessert looks like gunpowder, but don't be fooled! This gunpowder is a sweet treat.

Makes 4 servings

Ingredients:
- 10 chocolate sandwich cookies
- 2 cups milk
- 1 box instant pudding mix
- whipped topping

Tools:
- zip-top plastic bag, snack or sandwich size
- rolling pin
- liquid measuring cup
- clean, empty jar with lid
- 4 small bowls
- spoon

1 Put cookies in a zip-top plastic bag. Seal the bag.

2 Use a rolling pin to crush the cookies into tiny bits. Set aside.

3 Measure milk and add to a jar. Then add pudding mix to the jar.

4 Tightly close the jar. Shake it for two minutes.

5 Pour the pudding into four bowls. Let sit a few minutes.

6 Add a spoonful of whipped topping to each bowl. Then sprinkle with crushed cookies.

11

Scurvy Soup

Many pirates died from **scurvy** during long trips at sea. They didn't know that fruits with vitamin C could keep them healthy. This fruit soup would have been a tasty scurvy cure!

Makes 2 servings

Ingredients:
- 1 cup orange juice
- 1 cup apple juice
- 1 teaspoon lemon juice
- ½ cup vanilla nonfat yogurt
- 1 teaspoon honey
- 1 banana
- 1 cup raspberries, washed
- ½ cup crushed pineapple

Tools:
- liquid measuring cup
- measuring spoons
- mixing bowl
- measuring cups
- whisk
- 2 cereal bowls
- fork
- ladle

1 Measure and pour orange, apple, and lemon juices into a mixing bowl.

2 Measure yogurt and honey and add to the bowl. Whisk ingredients together.

3 In each cereal bowl, mash half of a banana with a fork.

4 Measure and add ½ cup raspberries and ¼ cup pineapple to each bowl.

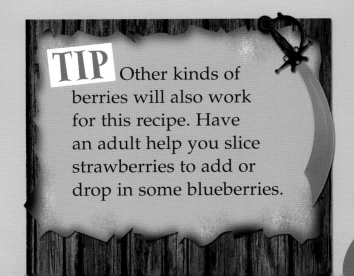

5 Use a ladle to pour the juice mixture over the fruit.

TIP Other kinds of berries will also work for this recipe. Have an adult help you slice strawberries to add or drop in some blueberries.

Peg-Leg Pickles

Sometimes a pirate lost a leg in a battle. Then he would have to use a wooden peg as a leg. These pickle rolls have peg legs of their own.

Makes 10 pickle rolls

Ingredients:
- 5 ham slices
- 1 tub whipped cream cheese, 8 ounces
- 10 baby pickles

Tools:
- cutting board
- butterknife
- spoon
- toothpicks

1 On a cutting board, use a butterknife to cut a piece of ham in half.

2 Use a spoon to spread a thin layer of cream cheese on the ham.

3 Lay a pickle at the short edge of the ham.

4 Roll the ham around the pickle.

5 Stick a toothpick into the outside of the pickle roll.

6 Repeat steps 1 through 5 to make more peg-leg pickles.

Blackbeard's Breakfast

The pirate Blackbeard was known for **plundering** ships. He probably took the breakfast right from people's hands. This waffle sandwich is worth fighting for.

Makes 1 sandwich

Ingredients:
- 2 toaster waffles
- 1 tablespoon peanut butter
- 1 tablespoon grape jelly

Tools:
- toaster
- plate
- measuring spoons
- butterknife

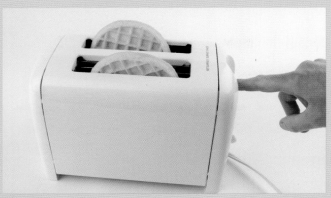

1 Have an adult help you heat two waffles in a toaster.

2 Carefully remove the hot waffles and put them on a plate.

3 Measure peanut butter. Use a butterknife to spread peanut butter on one waffle.

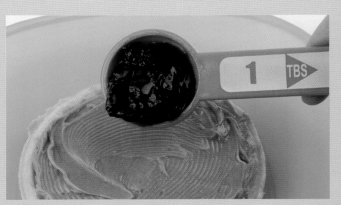

4 Measure jelly and spread it over the peanut butter.

5 Put the waffles together like a sandwich.

17

Sea Swords

Swords were popular with pirates. These celery stick swords will help you fight off hunger. **Makes 8 swords**

Ingredients:
- 1 can tuna, packed in water, 5 ounces
- ¼ cup light mayonnaise
- 8 pre-cut celery sticks, washed
- small fish-shaped crackers

Tools:
- can opener
- strainer
- small bowl
- mixing bowl
- measuring cups
- fork
- plate
- spoon

1 Ask an adult to open a can of tuna. Use a strainer to drain water into a small bowl.

2 Put tuna into a mixing bowl.

3 Measure mayonnaise and add to bowl. Use a fork to mix the mayonnaise and tuna.

4 Place celery sticks on a plate. Spread tuna mixture in the center of the celery sticks with a spoon.

5 Top each celery stick with fish-shaped crackers.

TIP Pirates had one thing right. Eating fish is very healthy.

Parrot Punch

Pirates saw parrots while sailing in **tropical** areas. This fruity punch will make you feel tropical all year long.

Makes 1 drink

Ingredients:
- ½ cup lemonade
- ½ cup pineapple juice
- ½ cup ginger ale
- ice cubes

Tools:
- liquid measuring cup
- glass
- spoon

1 Measure and pour lemonade, pineapple juice, and ginger ale into a glass.

2 Stir juices together with a spoon.

3 Add ice cubes to glass.

TIP Planning a party? Use 2 cups of each liquid and pour into a pitcher or punchbowl.

Glossary

cannon (KAN-uhn)—a large, heavy gun that uses gunpowder to fire large metal balls

galley (GAL-ee)—the kitchen on a ship or boat

gangplank (GANG-plangk)—a short bridge or piece of wood used for walking onto and off of a ship

ingredient (in-GREE-dee-uhnt)—an item used to make something else

plunder (PLUHN-dur)—to steal things by force, often during a battle

scurvy (SCUR-vee)—a disease caused by not getting enough vitamin C

spyglass (SPYE-glass)—a small telescope that makes faraway objects appear larger and closer

swab (SWAB)—to mop the floor or clean something

tropical (TROP-uh-kuhl)—having to do with the hot and wet areas near the equator

Read More

Fauchald, Nick. *Holy Guacamole!: and Other Scrumptious Snacks.* Kids Dish. Minneapolis: Picture Window Books, 2008.

Wilkes, Angela. *First Cooking Activity Book.* London: Dorling Kindersley, 2008.

Internet Sites

FactHound offers a safe, fun way to find Internet sites related to this book. All of the sites on FactHound have been researched by our staff.

Here's all you do:

Visit *www.facthound.com*

Type in this code: 9781429653756

Super-cool stuff! Check out projects, games and lots more at **www.capstonekids.com**

Index